Robots Don't Wear Sunscreen

Written by Eric Mills
Illustrated by Taillefer Long

Copyright © 2012, Taillefer Long, LLC dba ILLUMINATED STORIES, All rights reserved.

Published by: ILLUMINATED STORIES

info@illuminatedstories.com

Eric Mills & Taillefer Long

ISBN: 0984876200
ISBN-13: 978-0-9848762-0-4

DEDICATION

Robots Don't Wear Sunscreen is dedicated to beach goers and outdoor lovers everywhere. Our hope is to help educate people about the risks of sun exposure.

Sunburn hurts, but it is easy to prevent! Simple measures can make all the difference, and a small amount of sunscreen goes a long way.

This book is a fun and easy way of introducing children to the benefits of sunscreen. Always remember to wear plenty of it in the sun, and remind your friends and family to do so as well.

**Take this story as a lesson learned,
If you're heading outside don't get burned!**

Follow Jake and Ilene's advice:
**"When you hit the beach,
keep that sunscreen within reach!"**

www.SunscreenforRobots.com

ACKNOWLEDGMENTS

We are grateful for the support of our friends and family throughout this project, as well as the special contributions of Jesse Warnock, Karin Mills and many others whose efforts helped make this production a success. Special thanks to Angus Long for always being there to offer encouragement and brotherly advice.

According to the FDA:

If used as directed, with other sun protection measures, sunscreen reduces the risk of skin cancer and early skin aging, and helps prevent sunburn.

Jake and Ilene, two robots in love,
wanted to do something fun.

"On a beautiful day such as this,"
they thought,
"It'd be nice to get out in the sun."

So they gathered their toys,
their blankets and chairs,
Excited one thousand percent.

Everything needed for a day on the beach,
so off to the beach they went.

A dip in the water, a game on the beach,
life couldn't get any better.

The air was crisp, the sand was soft,
and the water, it had never been wetter.

For hours they played
in the sun and the sand,
but later ran into bad luck.

Ilene couldn't move, unable to roll,
her front wheel was rusted and stuck.

Too much time in the sun,
too much time in the sand,
had left Ilene stuck in her tracks.

Oil they needed to make her wheel roll,
but oil they forgot to pack.

"She's too heavy to carry,
and unable to move."
Jake knew what had to be done.

Go get some oil, fix Ilene's wheel,
and get his friend out of the sun.

With no oil shops close,
none nearby at all,
and his money pretty much spent,

Jake would have to search for oil,
so off on his search he went.

He came across a big man,
with a moustache and a hat,

Who had a little girlfriend
rubbing oil on his back.

Surely, he thought,
they'd have oil to spare for his friend,
who was stuck in the sun.

So he approached the man,
smiled, shook his hand,
and politely asked him for some.

"I wish I could help,"
the man said to Jake,
"To dislodge the wheel on Ilene."

"But oil I have none,
all I have is this,
and robots don't wear sunscreen."

So Jake carried on down the beach
on his quest,
and saw children playing in the sand.

And next to a boy building sandcastles,
was a girl with some oil in her hand.

"I'm sorry, poor robot,"
the girl held up her hand.
"I don't know what you think you've seen."

"This stuff only works
for humans with skin.
Robots don't wear sunscreen."

Jake began to worry,
but continued his search,
frightened of what might happen.

When he then came across
an old fishing boat,
and a man that looked like its captain.

"Excuse me sir!"
Jake yelled to the captain,
in order to get his attention.

The captain came over,
a fine looking man,
with a mighty fine beard,
I should mention.

He explained what had happened
and the captain felt bad saying,
"Oil? No, I have not."

He had just one bottle
that looked like some oil and said,
"This is the closest I've got."

"I use this lotion to protect my head,
from the bright and scorching sunbeams.

But it couldn't help you
because your head is metal…
Robots don't wear sunscreen."

Oil, it seems, is a hard thing to find
at the beach on a sunny, warm day.

That's when Jake heard some music
on the pier and thought,
"Maybe there's oil that way."

Jake had grown tired,
but had to push on
as the music began to grow near.

"What will become of Ilene,"
he thought,
"If I can't find oil on the pier?"

So up he went and away he asked
to everyone that could hear.

But no one had oil on the boardwalk
it seemed,
as he got to the end of the pier.

Now Jake was scared,
about to give up,
and head back down to the sand.

When all of a sudden,
he noticed the song
that was coming from the band.

Just as Jake had lost hope,
and his day nearly spoiled,
the band played their best number,
"Use The Sunscreen As Oil."

"Use the sunscreen as oil!
Sunscreen's as good as oil!
Your skin don't burn and
your blood don't boil,
but you can use the sunscreen as oil!"

"Use the sunscreen as oil!
Sunscreen's as good as oil!
I don't know where you're-a-gonna get it,
but use the sunscreen as oil!"

"That's it! That's it!"
Jake knew what to do,
and now he started cruisin'.

Off of the pier and back down to the beach,
to get some of that sunscreen they're usin'.

As fast as he could,
he ran down to the beach
to get himself some of that lotion.

And there was the captain,
right where he had left him,
next to his boat by the ocean.

"I can't give you all,
but can surely spare most,
because I live close to the store that sold it.

So here you are my fine metal friend,
and a new container to hold it."

A great big thank you,
and a quick wave goodbye,
Jake was back on the way to his friend.

But there still was a problem,
there was not enough sunscreen,
to get Ilene's wheel moving again.

But lucky for Jake, he saw the same kids,
playing in the very same sand.

And the same little girl,
next to the same sandcastle,
still held the same sunscreen in hand.

"Great News! Great News!"
Jake yelled to the group,
and smiling he came up and said,

"I know that you have no oil to give,
but I can use your sunscreen instead!"

The whole group cheered for Jake and Ilene
as soon as they heard the great news.

So Jake held out his cup,
and the kids squirted in,
more sunscreen for Jake to use!

They said their goodbyes,
and Jake kept on his way
in order to save poor Ilene.

But looking down in his cup,
he thought to himself,
"I could use a bit more sunscreen."

**Now getting close,
wondering where to get more,
Jake thought of one last place.**

**To the blanket and chair of the big man,
with the hat and moustache on his face.**

As he arrived, the man looked at Jake,
and then looked down in Jake's cup.

"So you *can* use sunscreen as oil!"
he proclaimed,
and proceeded to fill it right up.

A big thanks to the big man,
for saving the day,
and just like that Jake was gone.

Back to where Ilene was stalled,
to put the sunscreen on.

"I hope that this works," Jake thought to himself, Ilene near fainted and hot.

"Let's see if this lotion called sunscreen, can be used by a metal robot."

Onto the wheel the lotion was poured,
both of them very concerned.

They nervously waited for it to seep in,
and suddenly, Ilene's wheel turned!

"It worked! It worked!"
They cheered and they laughed,
quickly moving to get out of the sun.

So grateful was Jake for the sunscreen,
that he tried some on just for fun!

Excited and smiling and very relieved,
Ilene hugged Jake and Jake hugged Ilene.

"It took me all day,"
he said as her wheel rolled,
"To find out robots DO wear sunscreen!"

About the Author & Illustrator

ERIC MILLS

Eric Mills is a New Jersey native who grew up realizing the important power of literature in every phase of our lives. An avid Dr. Suess reader as a youngster, with children's books playing an important role in his upbringing--both in terms of mental development and family life--Mills learned to appreciate how poetic rhythm and colorful illustration can effectively engage young readers.

He combines this passion with his discovery and love of the South Carolina coast, his new home, in his first book, **Robots Don't Wear Sunscreen**. A graduate of Miami University of Ohio, Mills is a naturalist with expert knowledge of South Carolina coastal ecology. He continues to write books for youth from his home in Charleston, SC.

TAILLEFER LONG

Taillefer Long was raised in Florence, Italy, and Paris, France, until high school, when he relocated to the good ol' US of A. His artwork was first published while attending the University of North Carolina at Chapel Hill, as editorial cartoonist for the Daily Tar Heel. Since then, Taillefer has been a freelance illustrator, graphic designer, and cartoonist. His portfolio includes many children's books. Working in both traditional and digital media, he has branched out to offer full pre-publishing services.

Nicknamed "Cara de Leche" (Milk Face) by his Spanish-speaking friends, Taillefer understands the importance of sunscreen better than most. He lives and works in Charleston, SC but travels frequently to Italy, thanks to his mobile workstation.

For more examples of Taillefer's work go to: www.illuminatedstories.com

www.ingramcontent.com/pod-product-compliance
Lightning Source LLC
LaVergne TN
LVHW072052070426
835508LV00002B/68